LETTER TO MY CONCERNS

1

Dedicated to

Mathias Ikojo Moses

Table of Content:

BAD GOVERNMENT

4

Before now, it is an obvious activity

Political system of the country is rigorously managed.

Persons have no reasonable points for politics

As comparism is an essential feature

In ascertaining the propagative and deplorable level of government,

We have plenty to point attentions to.

All that have happened do have effects of divergent areas

Nigeria government is full of political rigmarole.

It has been from time immemorial

And what I can see in this present government

If far beyond the previous government and I equally

Think of so to the subsequent governments.

This government does not in one way to the other

Possesses good feature of politics.

The major achievements and legacies

The present administration have is retaliation and injustice of a highest level.

I wonder why God have chosen to leave us for a while!

There is no single democratically guidelines.

In politics, goodies and badies, prevails and avails

Depending on the actors and the time.

Under a government which seventy percent of citizens

Are very angry for hunger, there is a problem.

The government who is not capable enough

To preach togetherness of the family

Rather of eagerness to drop all who seem to correct

Within the family-hood and the against family-hood.

There are no essential platforms to discuss effectively.

All essential roads into the government for good constructions

Have been closed with happiness.

The reign of the government now is very obdurate.

All who built up the government and all

Who built up courage for better leadership

Are sky-rocked and stereotyped in their numbers and plans.

The government is very good in placing people

Whose the citizens have not placed interest on.

The government is good in using the originally bad-hearted ones.

But I wonder a day the government will change

Then, the citizens shall be granted second-phase of freedom.

What we must know is that,

The beginning marks the end.

So, very soon the government will be captured like a daydream.

Then we will have full colours of our politicians.

Though, no one is good,

But, there are some who are better to others.

At times, their drama is beyond comprehension.

But, within themselves, they are friendly.

They make public distractions

To simply and completely aids confusion

While they have full opportunity to exploit in the moment.

They have made politics a compulsory subject

For all individuals without interest.

The dullards among the citizens continue in the subject

Till the last breath and it rendered them very poor status.

Our politicians send their children abroad

To learn how to be smarter and intelligent

More than the citizens so as to have clear roads

To replace their parents position to continue the oppressions.

And I wonder why the citizens and the country-based

Have developed little-mind by saying,

They are more intelligent, knowledgeable to those who study abroad.

Some who have lost their memory thought that,

They are more intelligent and productive to the white ones!

What a shameful utterances!

In a country where all things are done on bad platforms

How could there be possibilities of good products?

The issue of age affidavit and the affidavits of other kinds,

The issue of taking formal education as the only means and not learning,

The issue of pardon of illegalities without a touch of punishment,

The issue of political instabilities,

The issue of not identifying oneself,

The issue of photocopies of lifestyles and characters,

The issue of supreme immunities at various levels,

The issue of bad constitution with it amendments

And the host in semblance,

Have brutally and absolutely placed the country

Under destruction without a surviving route.

All approaches used in controlling the affairs of the country

Are majorly useless and meaningless.

But, I still have a dream that,

One day, my nation will have similar seat

With some acclaimed nations of the earth

Through our tireless efforts of contributions

To make her seat where she needs to seat.

All individuals of the nation should start

The contributions without waiting for others

As humans are pregnant of divergent interests.

This will be possible if we can start emulating

The lives of the great men in history.

The country is so blessed

And together, we can make her a good dream

For all nations of the world.

I am taking a composary self-exile

So as to go for self fortification

To return for the change of the country.

I must return to make more unity in the househood

As I cant join the present team.

What you can't control becomes your master.

And I can't entertain the person to be my master.

I promise to bring all the popular products of the

Nation back home for restoration and reformative purpose.

I single-handedly detached myself

From all things that the country put much interest on

Because, I have seen that all those things ,

Are not handled as expected

And I am not under any obligation to state reasons.

For now, I can only preach for good emulations.

Go by whatever is profitable.

We should stop deceiving ourselves in all angles.

We should make sure to form good team

For the betterment of the country and the host alike.

TO YOU

My brother, presently, you have succeeded in one step

Forward to success as the country demands.

But, you must not lose you're her to that.

With experiences gathered so far,

I have solid ground to tell you to put more effort.

Now, you have done what ordinary people do.

Now, you are to begin journey of oneself which is success.

Though, I congratulate your efforts in that domain.

I have been with you and we are into one another.

So, I have conceived your impregnated heart towards success.

You are a good and large giver;

That has encouraged me enough to register

My concern towards your success in life.

The world is waiting for someone like you.

It is not our essential character to trust or believe

Someone or a friend, but, I do believe you

And that gave birth to realizing some of my hidden

Activities and principles to you. I salute you.

Therefore, for now, there are some things you need to leave.

Within ourselves, we know what is bad and good to us

And we know what to do to bring goodies to us.

I do enjoin you to learn and think of that.

Uniqueness is very good in accelerating success.

So, try to be self-principled and self-disciplined.

Put away all childish characters if you think you have.

Refuse to internal and external distractions henceforth.

Emulate the lives of great people.

Divert your focus and interest from people.

Be your second-owner after God.

Do make your people happy occasionally

So that you can also get happiness at times.

Put trust in God and do things on good calculations.

Continue to be generous as you always do.

Create better space for God to others in your heart.

Do try to understand the secret of failures, challenges and stagnation.

Do also to patience, handiwork and diligent, please.

The fastest road towards any place in life is spirituality;

Try to be spiritual as nothing can appear physical

Without spiritual transactions and manipulations.

I believe in your struggles!

I believe in your characters!

I believe in your faith!

And I believe in our God!

See us at the top!

I put interest in you simply for the good knowledge

Of your past records and the present characters exhibited.

I do urge you for the continuation, please.

In this present generation where dynamism is a high subject

We have plenty characters that tagged a lady

For a wife-ship candidacy. That is very true.

Don't think men are the same.

Remember that we all have our different interest

In pursuing whatever ought to be our concern.

I am ever harmless. So, I might be good to you.

Ladies take relationship as a fatal and final phenomenon

But love which is the product of relationship

Matter most in all angles of life.

No one can cheat love but can cheat relationship

Therefore, relationship should be given attention as deserved

Intelligent ladies will know of this

But, smart ladies can't know all about this!

Intelligent matter most in relationship to smartness

And emotions and feelings matter most in love than intelligent.

Remember, someone is loved according to how he or she deserved.

Your interest of love determines the result of your love.

Love whosoever you love and like whosoever you like.

Don't allow situations and reasons determine your love

Because the both don't last forever but love exist forever.

Expect strange different things from me as you have

Met a great man the world is currently celebrating.

Love do not have hidden channel to the heart.

Love is the neutralizer of all kinds of mind,

Love is not a hidden subject and phenomenon and

For these, our relationship is declared open.

Get ready for challenges, temptations and problems.

Great love experiences the above.

Endurance is the best keeper of love.

Therefore, try to keep to this in order to experience

The designed content and dividend of the love.

Before now, you have met plenty guys.

Opportunity to meet plenty people is as the same as

Meeting plenty characters and meanings of life.

I am not the same as they are as usual

Simply for exhibiting different characters as well.

Life with me and outside me is very good and simple.

I treat all humans equally but I slightly reserved

For as many that might come with dirty minds.

Get this so that you might not be confused on me.

May God help us!

I own you all my apologies.

You are a rare vessels and domain.

I thought originality is a far journey.

You taught me very better and deeper about originality of ladies.

My previous apparatus in identifying original ladies

Have been put to shame. I salute your lessons!

My respect for you remains higher forever.

I treated you less-valued to your level of value.

With your intelligent submission, I am rebranded.

I pray for more open doors after this.

Do you think I will ever forget or reject you?

I do not possess such childish character.

For giving me good lessons about ladies,

I own you a promise of putting your status higher in feminism.

Don't reason our relationship to be accidental.

It has been my desire and you have satisfied the desire.

By meeting a great man, you are now great.

You have given me the desire of my interest

And I shall by God's grace give you yours with short time.

My profound appreciations to your family for the sake of your life.

Your kind gestures remain ever fresh in my memories.

God bless us!

I never know the present generation has your product.

You are a rare type and I love your lifestyle.

You have an effective knowledge and intelligent

Simply for understanding better and deeper about

The school of realism and the school of idealism.

My best knowledge of appreciation goes to your family.

You taught me plenty things about believing in others.

So, I remain ever grateful to your kind gestures.

You aid my stay in Lokoja comfortable.

You have taken me as your blood elder brother.

Good life never fades; therefore, you will not fade.

Continue in your dedicated character for your exploit.

You have given me good lessons on good platform.

And I am sure within myself that, I will give you lesson.

The level we have attained in understanding so far,

Our fervent prayers is for long life so as to contribute

Our quarter to the betterment of humanity by His grace.

Be prayerful about your lifestyle; because, your success

Come directly from characters and you have gotten it

That is why I enjoin you to be prayerful for it continuation.

I respect you higher at knowing our incumbent

Position in the family. Then, I concluded on your greatness.

I have learnt from your courage more than mine.

Your eminent study of hope and future

Within yourself and others around you should be the

Best subject of all who are still in the school of struggle.

It should be the security of the present situation.

Extending the similar study to others should

Be your prominence assignment if only you are

Demanding for enabling environment.

Heaven and earth shall celebrate you!

I salute your existence.

God help us all!

Age has no effect in whatever that has bigger effect.

Life is best qualified with contents and not in numbers.

Numbers are for children schools while

Contents are the focus learning of adults.

Once you know what you are up to, be focused

And shun all talks that might discourage you.

We all have different purpose and desires in life.

Are you foolish enough to live by others' own to forget yours?

Be wise then so that you enjoy speedy movement

In accomplishing your purposes and manifesting your desires.

Lifespan on earth is too short to seize

 A whole day listening to people without personal thinking.

What can decorate your life is a product of your desire.

In life, before you can attain you desires,

You must know that you are different from others.

So, try to be unique to fast rack your purpose in life.

I do forever respect and emulate your courage.

You have good outer characters

Try to have the same inside for good home.

You own your life after God.

So, give time to God and give yourself time as well.

Then your success is a sure idea.

May God help us!

If you pick five guys at a moment, you might miss all,

If you pick four, you might marry the worst one,

If you pick three, you might marry the bad one,

If you pick two, you might marry good one and,

If you pick one, you might marry the better one,

And remember that you can't marry the best one

As God is our best husband and wife.

Never abort pregnancy for anyone you want to marry

No matter the condition of the presence.

Make it a sacrifice so that the existence

Of the child can make you free.

Never love with condition. This kills before time.

I will take you as one of my female best friend

Simply for having this philosophy, "not neglecting anyone".

It is written all over you about your greatness.

The kind gestures you have given me have confirmed your greatness.

Words are the only thing to register appreciations, if not,

I will not be satisfied using words to convey my gratitude to you.

All I wish you is the best of luck

In all things you do.

Uniqueness is the benchhall of greatness.

Bad uniqueness is bad greatness and the same to good.

Uniqueness is always a subject of goodness.

This can never disappoint someone except a fool.

Point to a unique life and I tell you about success.

Grace and mercy is labeled on uniqueness.

Tangible growth and development of an environment

Come from the genuine work of uniqueness.

This shows the real beauty of life.

The birth of Jesus Christ is the genesis of divine love

And may the love behind the birth and all it concerns

Speedily speak for you in all angles of your life as the

World marks the anniversary today, so that, now and

Subsequently, you shall gain global celebration as He

Has gained.

The birth of Jesus Christ symbolizes laughter as all

In its concerns and contents connote and denote happiness,

Therefore, as today marks the remembrance, laughter shall

Be the order of the day in your life. So, as the

World celebrates the birthday anniversary of Jesus Christ,

You shall also gain global celebration of your life.

The birth of Jesus Christ gave birth to grace and mercy.

And as He was born for your sake, the prime

Reasons behind His birth shall speedily speak for you,

Now and forever as we record the anniversary. All your

Desires shall see lives under sun and you shall gain

Global celebration on the basis of the remembrance.

The birth of Jesus Christ marks the end of our struggles

And for that sake, from now till the last day, your

Struggles are over as the potential reasons behind His birth

Shall begin to speedily speak for you over all your concerns

At all angles, so that, you can gain global celebration as He has gained.

Happy Christmas!

New Year symbolizes joy

As all that it connotes and denotes is happiness

Which is simply celebration of advancement.

Each year carries new and strange packages.

But the only opportunity to gain yours

Speak highly on the availability of love.

Though, love is immeasurable, but, the quality of love

You give out determines the quality in return.

You can never see good love if you don't give out good love;

The same happen in the opposite.

So, make good love the entrance of the year.

Set apart all that can't grant your success.

Do away with approaches that can't manifest your plans.

Abscond from whatever that can't motivate your dream, then,

Your success shall be channeled in relevance to the

Advancement of days throughout this good year and

The world in her masses, will celebrate you.

We should all dwell in the praises of God.

There will be no enlargement without praises.

It is better to praise than to pray.

Praises exalt the name of God.

This is the work for God while prayer

Is a work for personal growth.

Remember, if you can take God first,

All your wishes become effectual prayers.

Character is a golden name of humans

Once you are entitled to good character

You are at the peak of life.

Human can only be celebrated by character

Character is what affects others

Whatever you have outside this is for personal security

Because whatever a man has in life

Is achieved on the bases of character.

It is a universal law that,

Good characters attract good things

While the opposite attract it kinds.

Life is not balance with prayers and praises

When good character is not involved.

Note that, prayer and praises help human during lifetime

But character guarantee internity

And appropriate use of life on earth.

This happens simply for a fact that both of them

Possess different works and spirits.

There is no time to play on earth

As life is very short.

You might play to confirm the law of nature

But you must not play for the whole day.

Serious life always dies at an appropriate time

Their life might be short or long

But, all they are here for is always achieved:

Remembering that long days do not count

But the few days count with effects.

If a serious man dies quickly, he has either

Reached his dream or has handed over his dream for others

And if a serious man lives longer, he has not quickly

Reached his limit of dream or purpose.

Therefore, a serious mind dies happily for fulfilling a dream.

But unserious man either experience long or short life

With confusion and struggles without reasonable meanings.

Their lives decrease other peoples' lives.

And that is the worst of all kinds.

We have to be serious in all things that is good.

This will only give our lives meanings

Either we leave it in a short or long time.

The first day of each year remains the same

The packages are different

That is why we must continually changing our character

Until it become better enough to receive our packages.

This can happen with plenty things:

Starting from our characters to approaches.

Only when the both become appropriate;

The packages do not have sight to locate you.

Therefore, we should be highly mindful of the both;

In order to be among the partaker of the year's goodies.

A life become meaningful when your characters

And approaches become reasonable.

The final thing to note every New Year is that,

Only when your mind is filled up with joy to

Bring the effects of your success to others,

Free expressway for manifestation of dream is acquired.

Take it in mind that,

The only reason behind a dream is to comfort others

Not necessarily me as I don't have long days on earth.

I do assure you of your success

By leaving in harmony to all these, then,

The destiny of your characters and approaches become useful.

Happy New Year!

We should think primely during the day

When shadow and light help humans

During the dark time, things appears nearer

Simply as darkness do deceive people.

During the day time, things appears far

Simply as light give careful advices

No human strength can supersede the power of darkness

Rather the strength of light

Humans and light are far from one another

So as humans and darkness are far from one another.

What connect humans and light is grace and obedience

And what connect humans and darkness is wish and disobedience

Therefore, we should always make promises during the day

As promises are normally fulfilled during the day.

Those who can produce result effectively and effectually

During the dark times are very special and extraordinary in such areas

Don't over play during the both times

As both of them are productive

Both times are essentials

But what happen much during the times give an account

The relationship between the both is not funny.

Humans need to be careful all times

As whatever is highly projected during the night appears before during the day

So, they sometimes exchanges season of results

And there do not that at times.

Strive better to know more about the both

In order not to be victim of their different understanding

I give kudos to the both time in life.

You are an excellent adviser.

Simply because you keep all in his or her good places.

Understand so much about race of life.

It is a better idea to impact whatever good you know

Because the very kind of you is the same for others.

Your personality is up to your kindness

That is why you are recommended for others.

I do appreciate everything done so far.

You are greatly great for helping great people.

This is your nature and I hope this will help you.

I have greatly enjoyed you for this short period

And we shall enjoy one another for the life time.

We do have reasons for whatever we do.

We pray for the reason to help our purpose in life.

One of the greatest things we must not do is hatred.

Hatred is the mother of all evils.

Hatred at any level and time never bring goodies to a life.

This is one of the deadliest diseases without drugs.

Hatred simply means dark minds towards pictures.

The power of hatred supersedes the power of death.

It is better to develop death theories to the theories of hatred

Because, death is meaningful but hatred is not.

What on earth is more painful than hatred?

A lifetime symptoms of poverty and untimely death.

A life nurtured by hatred can never amount to anything in life.

Therefore, I enjoin all who dwell in it to abscond

Before it is too late for the reversal.

But, good wish and concentration

Is the father of all goodies.

With such mindset, the world is yours.

This has no single factor

All external factors that might come should be neglected

The essential spirits behind this ever supernatural.

Good wish and concentration is a high channel of love.

This give birth to long-life as grace

Is the higher dividend in the pursuit.

These are the two predominant pursuits in human's life

There are daily investments to the future

And make sure, yours is a good one.

And we should note that, behind any plan and mission

Lies between good and evil.

That is why sensitivities to natures are highly important.

Therefore, only the fool wants to see the effects of time

Before he can value it.

And we must be careful for no one understands the wisdom of God.

Because a child that dies early sees he has nothing to do on earth.

We have day and nigh

So as we have longer days and nights, so as we have shorter days and nights.

Both good and evil men experience longer days and nights.

This happens whenever progress is dormant or stagnated.

At times, when some people are experiencing longer days

And nights is at time of troubles

While some is the opposite.

Days and nights remain as they are.

People inside make it longer and shorter.

Only what changes are seasons and times.

Because, natures changes seasons and times.

Humans must be in a good condition with natures

In order to experience good seasons and times.

Humans need to be flexible with approaches to meet up goals

In order not to experience either

Longer days and nights or shorter days and nights.

What affect either longer days or nights

Is when someone fails to take up responsibilities and duties

As he becomes an element of play for the sake

Delays arrive until he or she starts to take up those things.

And the better chances to overcome this when

Learning is acknowledged as the father of experience

As one who refuses to learn can never achieve adequate experience;

Be happy with good changes of others even if the changes

Hurt or do no favour to you; holding to back and living

By complaining is the best principle of failure to those times and seasons;

And to largely remember that, the very possible solution of humans

Problems at those times and seasons lies behind the maturity

Put in place of patience and reasoning.

Life is very deceiving and that is why,

You must be careful and sensitive

As at times, it divert human attention

From where things are not concerned of.

Some things are meant to be whatever happens

Some things are not meant to be whatever happens

That is why we can say

Only God knows our end point.

We only struggle for living when life has an option

But whenever life seems to enjoy, option become useless

Option creates ways for solidarity and more perfection

In most cases, living life of an option is the first stage

It is a necessary part for some people.

If you seem to be inclusive, try to make it your consultant.

Life is not straight;

That is why life is very precious.

The dividend of life arise from the struggles of life

Struggles in life is inevitable

That is why factors of life originate from struggles

And struggles originates from plans

And plans originates from personality

And personality originates from dream

And dream originates from purpose.

Life is a monumental fact, it has no permanent base

It is a channel of communication is a doomed society;

As it creates factual adventures. For this,

Life is simple and interactive in nature.

That is why, in a society where this is not observed,

We have very high rate of difficulties in all angles.

This is very important and should be noted

For easy and betterment of humanity.

In life, if you lack understanding

You have definitely lack character

And if you lack the both,

You have wholistically lost everything.

As this happens, you live in doom

Until you have accepted to give it a possible trial.

So you must not lose understanding of your life

Even if you may lose anything.

Your understanding has better work to do in your personality.

Life owns you nothing rather you own life.

And the possibility of achieving this account for adequate consideration of above

Though we have no reason to attend to all,

But even the few people you are to attend to needs them.

Life is difficult and easy on the both grounds.

These are to be taken with prime priority

To aid clear and simple manifestation of our purpose.

Plenty things are hidden in life for the sake of poor delivery

The best we can do about this is to be simpler than our approaches

In delivery our earthly purpose.

The easiest way to corrupt our earthly purpose is comparism

Once a life is open to comparism, it is ready for struggles

That are not attached to it existence and hereby causes delay.

A compared life is definitely uncompleted life.

Comparism is the bench-hall of struggles and

Struggles are liable to failures

And if such person is not courageous enough,

The purpose can be completely ruined

As failures handled carelessly is liable to defeat.

Whatever that might not allow us to complete our purpose

Is capable to steal our joy and happiness here and hereafter

And such thing should be dealt with ultimate seriousness.

I am most happy for the welcome

You believe in your son, which is why

You do believe me as well.

We are very sure to deliver believe labeled on us.

With your medieval brain,

Attempt to gather little wealth is possible and

I can never tell what we will use our contemporary brain for!

What I do know is that, if parent can do well,

The children should do better.

The most enduring fact is emulation.

Our styles and level of emulation should be superficial

That is why we have better chances.

The world is demanding our attention and for that reason

You can see us exhibiting and displaying some characters

That is very out of your experience.

Believe should be the better account given to your loved ones

Though the betrayal of nowadays is very plenty

But one must believe himself and others around him

In order to have joyful moments.

If we should take instances from many angles of life,

It is very difficult to tag someone with believe

But the only pregnancy for the future is believe,

Believe should be the ultimate deposit of future.

Future and believe are the best components of greatness.

We shall happily celebrate together

For honoring the major components of greatness.

Having chosen the divine direction,

Grace to long-life and prosperity to help us in life

Surely be our portion.

See us at the top!

I am very simple and understanding.

But I treat all humans as deserved.

You are not fully exposed to the world of reality

And realism as gotten by your approach.

This give birth to your unnecessary complains about life.

In life, there are some things that need not to be taught.

If you make yourself a subject of attraction

You might definitely see things that are not earlier

Earmarked in your expectations.

Only kids complain much on human actions.

The adults complain much on reasons behind actions.

At times, whatever similar people do to one another

On a devilish domain, is not meant to be judged.

Judgment is to be experienced

Whenever people of the different opposite status

Do that to one another.

Those who complain much are weak.

The weak are dangerous in a society.

Because, if you are strong, you are the hope of others.

No one is naturally weak or strong, human efforts make the both

The stronger are the marketable ones while

The weaker are the storms of life.

We learn plenty things from smartness but

Dull people are the subject of mockery and evil-deeds.

To be fruitful and heart-touching human,

You must take any type of risk and ways to name success.

Try to adapt to environments to see how to defeat situations

Possibly gaining ground of the new place.

We don't necessarily have shame in the beginning nor middle

But at the end, where hopes are almost lost.

Learn from people you need to learn from.

Make sure you have ways of manipulating things on yourself.

That strictly defines a personality.

May God help us!

You are a lady with industrious life.

Your life is meant to be emulated

By any focused and ready delivery purpose lady.

You place men as they deserve to be done.

I ever respect you for your characters.

If I should have little or few ladies to acknowledge

I will definitely have you as one.

With any single lady I do like,

I have some characters in her.

For yours: you are respectful, hand-working, intelligent,

You put hope where there are hopes.

You are good in making interactions.

You over-look where there are no necessaries.

Above all, you are busy making yourself available

To your creator while shunning the worldly things.

These characters will surely get you your desired place.

Always remember that, life is merciful to the gracious ones,

Life is free to the hand-working people,

Life is rude to the weak people

Therefore, be committed to whatever you like.

Treat all things with your heart desires.

Never look for excuses in life.

Try not to be an option.

Continue to maintain your status.

Only that will surely put you there by His grace.

We shall surely help ourselves as the worth is noted.

May God help us!

Shadrachology

Ideguology

Ojonugwaology

The World Changers Magazine

Discourse Analysis of Literature Genres

The Concepts

The Advanced Concepts

Poverty and Other Poems

The World of Trouble and Other Poems

Agent of Embezzlement and Other Poems

My Result

My Experience

A Day and Other Poems

Death and Other Poems

A Successful Family

Unexpected

A Choice

Stubborn Uncle

Divine Direction

A Great Stranger

Unexpected Change

The Childhood Colour and Other Short Stories

The Pride of A Family and Policy Reputation

Medicine for Stubbornness and The Return of Tradition

The Recalcitrant Pupil and The United

Letter to my Father

Letter to my Concerns

Constitution of Shadrach Group

The Works of Shadrachology

The Works of Shadrachology 2

The Works of Shadrachology 3

The Works of Shadrachology 4

The Works of Shadrachology 5